THEM

—— AND ——

US

THEM
— AND —
US

Compiled by Jennifer Curry
Illustrated by Susie Jenkin-Pearce

The Bodley Head
London

First published in 1993 by
The Bodley Head Children's Books
an imprint of Random House UK Ltd
20 Vauxhall Bridge Road, London SW1V 2SA

Random House Australia Pty Ltd
20 Alfred Street, Sydney, NSW 2061

Random House New Zealand Ltd
PO Box 40–086, Glenfield, Auckland 10, New Zealand

Random House South Africa Pty Ltd
PO Box 337, Bergvlei 2012, South Africa

Typeset by Deltatype Ltd, Ellesmere Port
Printed and bound in Great Britain
by Mackays of Chatham Plc, Chatham, Kent

A catalogue record for this book
is available from the British Library

ISBN 0–370–318234

CONTENTS

This book is dedicated
with love and thanks
to Carol and her family.

First Day at School

'I am not going!'
My mum grips my hand
Assuring that it's fun.
Suddenly!
Gates stare at me
That are bigger than my dad.
'Do they eat shredded wheat?'
They open
I walk in
Boys run about
Shouting.
A lady walks up.
'Whose mummy are you?' I say.
A bell rings,
Then a whistle blows.
Children walk in a big, big house.
Doors shut like prison gates.
My mummy's hand leaves mine
My last words are . . .
'Please look after teddy!'

Melanie Louise Skipper (11)

First Day

I kiss her goodbye.
Wondering –
Why do I feel
in the way?

Taking her hand
the teacher shows
her the books
and the sandpit.
Absorbed, she's
ready to play.

For myself, I am
ready to cry
for that daughter
of mine. Our time
I shall miss.

She looks round
and smiles.
The sun is so
bright. School
has begun and

I'm suddenly glad
this is her
first day.
See you later
I say.

Ann Bonner

First Lesson

The bike stands, glistening silver.
I climb on.
The cold sharp frame
Saws my leg
And the hard seat bites.
I start off –
Slowly at first,
With shaky wobbles.
I pedal faster.
'Huh! This cycling lark's
Real easy at the start.'
Then, with a jerk, my dad lets go.
Adrenaline changes my grin to a grimace.
I cannot stop for fear of falling.
Scared to turn my handle-bars,
I crash into a prickly bush;
A thorn punctures my skin.
I let out a yell of pain.
'Oh, don't be a baby,' says Dad.
'You made a good five yards.'

Andrew Storer (12)

Esmé on her Brother's Bicycle

One foot on, one foot pushing, Esmé starting off beside
Wheels too tall to mount astride,
Swings the off leg forward featly,
Clears the high bar nimbly, neatly,
With a concentrated frown
Bears the upper pedal down
As the lower rises, then
Brings her whole weight round again,
Leaning forward, gripping tight,
With her knuckles showing white,
Down the road goes, fast and small,
Never sitting down at all.

Russell Hoban

Lovely Tracey

Dear Tracey,
   I am sending
This letter to you
to show all my love
for you and care
and respect.
This letter is not
from Peter it is from
Someone in class
Two who cares and
loves you very much.
Perhaps one day
I may not like
you as much as I do
now so while you've
got some time to
show your love for
me just use it.
Don't be shy to say
it if you do I
will be really glad
to know that you
love me. I have
only one thing to
say in nearly
everything I do I
always think of you
my beautiful girl.
   From *David*

David Phipps (9)

Growing Pain

The boy was barely five years old.
We sent him to the little school
And left him there to learn the names
Of flowers in jam jars on the sill
And learn to do as he was told.
He seemed quite happy there until
Three weeks afterwards, at night,
The darkness whimpered in his room.
I went upstairs, switched on his light,
And found him wide awake, distraught,
Sheets mangled and his eiderdown
Untidy carpet on the floor.
I said, 'Why can't you sleep? A pain?'
He snuffled, gave a little moan,
And then he spoke a single word:
'Jessica.' The sound was blurred.
'Jessica? What do you mean?'
'A girl at school called Jessica,
She hurts –' he touched himself between
The heart and stomach '– she has been
Aching here and I can see her.'
Nothing I had read or heard
Instructed me in what to do.
I covered him and stroked his head.
'The pain will go, in time,' I said.

Vernon Scannell

A Swimming Song

We had a
smashing time, a splashing time,
a real wavywater time.

A
jumping time, a plunging time,
a fine underwater time.

I played chase, swam in a race,
Splashed my friend, in her face,
Touched the bottom, reached the top,
Swam until I could not stop,
Made little bubbles, whopping waves,
Pretended there were secret caves,
Swam a breaststroke, tried to crawl,
Could not swim on my back at all.
Feeling wet, soon be dry,
Towels, and clothes, then home we fly.

Sarah Ainsworth (11)

First Lesson

Lie back, daughter, let your head
be tipped back in the cup of my hand.
Gently, and I will hold you. Spread
your arms wide, lie out on the stream
and look high at the gulls. A dead-
man's float is face down. You will dive
and swim soon enough where this tidewater
ebbs to the sea. Daughter, believe
me, when you tire on the long thrash
to your island, lie up, and survive.
As you float now, where I held you
and let go, remember when fear
cramps your heart what I told you:
lie gently and wide to the light-year
stars, lie back, and the sea will hold you.

Philip Booth

Divali

Firework Festival

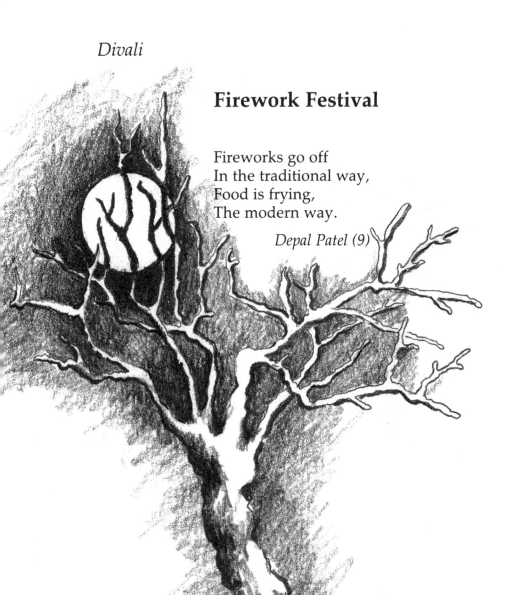

Fireworks go off
In the traditional way,
Food is frying,
The modern way.

Depal Patel (9)

Divali is a joyful new year festival celebrated by both Hindus and Sikhs with fireworks and sparklers. The people welcome Lakshmi, the goddess of good fortune, into their homes with colourful decorations and lighted lamps. They believe She will pass by any house that is not especially lit up in Her honour.

Divali

Winter stalks us
like a leopard in the mountains
scenting prey.

It grows dark,
bare trees stick black bars
across the moon's silver eye.

I will light my lamp for you
Lakshmi,
drive away the darkness.

Welcome you into my home
Lakshmi,
beckon you from every window

With light that blazes
out like flames
across the sombre sky.

Certain houses
crouch in shadow, do not hear
your gentle voice.

Will not feel
your gentle heartbeat
bring prosperity and fortune.

Darkness hunts them
like a leopard in the mountains
stalking prey.

David Harmer

Being Stuck in Goal

The goalie's ill,
Oh drat I'm in goal.
Just my luck.
I've got the wind blowing in my face,
The ground's water-logged and it's near enough
   snowing.

All the play has been at the other end.
My hands are like ice cubes,
I feel the bitter weather,
Biting off one toe at a time.
Only a few minutes left,
And,
Suddenly,
They break.
Their best player is leading the attack,
He's shooting,
I summon up all my energy and hurl myself
   across the goal,
Landing with a thud.
It knocks me breathless but I'm still clutching
   the ball,
Everybody was bundling me,
The team's hero.

Paul Oliffe (11)

One Girl to Nil

Zipper Zach zoomed up the pitch,
drew up sharply with a stitch,
disappeared under a scrum.
Scarce of air he went quite numb.

To the rescue came young Zeph
like the west wind, from the left,
wafted on in borrowed kit,
burst the blighters like a zit:

studded boots mashed blood with mud,
heads met others with a thud.
Zephyr sent their senses crashing,
scored a winner bully bashing,

dribbled off towards the goal
wobbling like a new-born foal,
wumphed the ball – her final kill.
Zach's team won: one girl to nil.

Gina Douthwaite

Hallowe'en

The witches fly in the moonlight,
with long dark purple cloaks
Streaming behind them.
The cackles and screams,
their black cats spitting
their chins almost touching their broomsticks,
I saw them on Hallowe'en.
Beyond the weird ghostly enchanted forest.
The wizards flying by the power
of their long black cloaks.
The trees with boughs bending
over you as if you
were prisoners of the wood.
The rushing rivers rushing
with the North Wind.
The fog spreading,
I saw all this on Hallowe'en.
The witches collecting
Fog and mist and midnight air.
Moonlight too.
The goblins, ghouls, sprites
trolls and pixies creeping
out of mossy damp green holes.
I saw all this from my bedroom window.
The spiders amongst
the twigs and branches of the trees
spinning webs.
Skeletons (Men) and ghosts (Ladys)
Walking together arm in arm.
I saw all this from my bedroom window.

Dawn Elizabeth Edwards (7)

Hallowe'en Games

The Hallowe'en children are out tonight,
casting spells in the murky gloom,
dressed as the grandest of ghosties and ghoulies.

On the doorstep neighbours are tricked
or treated (usually to some boring nursery rhyme)
and the estate comes alive with
hideous screams and terrifying torment,
well, pretend screams and just a touch of torment
when someone accidentally stood on the cat's paw.

The child's thrill of prowling wears off
as the night wears on
and the dull slam of the last door
finalises the evening's frights.

John Rice

Hallowe'en is the name we give to October 31st, which is All-hallows Eve or the Eve of All Saints' Day. On this night the dead are said to rise up out of their graves and walk about the earth. Children dress up, blacken their faces, make lanterns out of pumpkins or turnips, and wander about in the dark streets. They knock on doors demanding 'trick or treat'. Unless grown-ups give them some sort of little treat, they play a trick on them.

My Grandad

Grandad Lea
Was getting old.
He's gone to Baby Jesus
To help him do his stuff.

Matthew Lea (4)

Your Grandad Died

The day your Grandad died
I, father, cried and cried
To loose the sour salt inside.

But you remained dry-eyed,
No sign of tears, your Grandad's death defied,
All threat of grave denied.

At nine, eleven, my brave boys,
For you there was no mourning noise,
No waste of tearful breath.
For days you merely quietly sat
To silent sing his living,
Not his long-earned death.

John Kitching

Rockets

A match alight
A rocket racing into the air
And coming down in
rainbows of rage.

Jonathan Brown (7)

Firework Night

The sky is filled with sparks and flames;
the children rush about,
their cries are hardly heard among
the din of bangers, jumping jacks and rockets.

Dogs howl and cats cry –
Frightened of the noise.
The sky is filled with cordite smoke.
The fire is burning high.
Flashes here and crackles there.
A rocket soars into the sky.

Among all this noise nobody hears
a small child sobbing in the shade,
a banger exploded in his hand
and only he can feel the pain.

Eric Simpson

Going to Tea with Grandma

I'm going to tea with Grandma
I wonder what there'll be?
A big round cake with a cherry on top,
Some biscuits and a cup of tea.

I'm going to tea with Grandma
She asked me what I'd like.
Jelly perhaps and ice-cream too,
Oh what a lovely sight.

I'm going to tea with Grandma
I'll help her make the tea.
Then we'll sit down and eat it all,
Just Grandma and me.

Alexandra Calvert (7)

Grandchild

You are here.
Filling each room
with your laughter.
When you arrive
the quiet walls come
alive with the sound
of your voice.

Outside the dew
bloom of morning.
Brittle leaves fallen
with autumn take on
a new meaning.
The garden, a little
forlorn at this time
of year gives an ear to
the life that you bring.
Wakes up for a while.
Remembers the spring.

Stars now gleaming.
Moon streaming bright
through the shutters
of night hears your soft
snoring. Your mutters
of dreams as I write.
A storm wind is rising.
While it blows wild
sleep, my grandchild.

Ann Bonner

Hanukkah, The Festival of Oil

We walk in, happy and joyful,
The men wearing Kippahs
The ladies in black.
We start talking to each other.
We have a drink,
The ceremony begins.
A long speech starts,
About Hanukkah the festival of oil.
Everyone sings songs in Hebrew,
Then the children step forward
To light the candles.
We end the ceremony in silence.
The festival is of oil,
So we eat oily foods,
Doughnuts, peanuts and crisps.
We leave late at night,
With oil in our minds.

Laura Walker (9)

Hanukkah is a Jewish celebration, a festival of light. It lasts for eight days, and on each day a special candle is lit in a ceremonial candleholder called a menorah.

Eight Candles Burning

Three stars in the sky;
the children have counted them twice.
The menorah is polished,
the matches to hand,
ready to set a candle alight,
today, tomorrow and every night
until we see
                eight candles burning.

Bright as the stars,
the children's eyes and promises.
Parents, grandparents are children again,
thankful for freedom,
happy to set a candle alight,
today, tomorrow and every night
until we see
                eight candles burning.

Around the table
faces are glowing at stories retold.
Like the flame of the match
hearts are burning,
eager to set a candle alight,
today, tomorrow and every night
until we see
                eight candles burning.

Celia Warren

The School Nativity play

Christmas Joy

The audience, chilled from the frosty night
Fumbled into the stuffy hall.
Silver stars clung,
Tinsel was drooped around the cramped room.
They sat, not knowing what to expect
From a group of children wearing old curtains
And tinsel round their heads.
The hall grew warmer,
A light beamed on to a home-made crib.
A cloth was draped over Jesus' worn face.
Backstage everyone was excited,
Except me.
Hot and clammy, I sat in a corner
Waiting for my turn.
I was pushed on to the stage
And blinded.
My angel's costume was crumpled,
My face was numb.
I could see the Headmaster
Lounging in his plastic chair.
He gave a smile,
Urging me to speak.
One eye gave a friendly wink.
It was Christmas.

Helen Robinson (13)

Christmas Pageant

The third-grade angels, two by two,
March in, their cardboard wings askew.

A kindergarten shepherd skips;
A halo from its mooring slips.

The oriental kings, all three,
Wear Mama's costume jewellery,

While spotlights from each ribboned wreath
Accent the braces on the teeth,

And wise men, from the upper classes
Look *very* wise, in horn-rimmed glasses.

Margaret Fishback

Gone

When's he coming back Mam?
When's he coming home?
Why's he gone away Mam,
And left us all alone?

Why didn't you make him stay Mam?
It's Christmas in two weeks
He will be back before then
He's to mend the roof, it leaks.

Yes, I know he couldn't fix it
But it doesn't matter what he does
I don't mind if the roof caves in
As long as he's here with us.

Where's his big black boots Mam?
Where's his coat and hat?
When's he coming home Mam?
When's he coming back?

Ellen Jackson (12)

Split Family

When you came home from school
One day, your Mother wasn't there.
When she came home, I had to go.
I said, 'I hope you know I care.'

When you grow up, may you forgive –
And know that they were truly sad –
Your Monday–Friday part-time Mum,
Your seeming-cheerful weekend Dad.

John Kitching

Lucy's Carol

When the Baby borned
Joseph said to Mary,
'What am I going to do about
This Little-born Jesus Baby Christ?
I never knew it was going to be like
    this,
With all these angels and kings
And shepherds and stars and things;
It's got me worried, I can tell you,
On Christmas Day in the morning.'

Mary said to Joseph,
'Not to worry, my darling,
Dear old darling Joseph;
Everything's going to be all right,
Because the Angel told me not to fear;
So just hold up the lamp,
So I can see the dear funny sweet
    little face
Of my darling Little-born Jesus Baby
    Christ.'

Joseph said to Mary,
'Behold the handy-man of the Lord!'

Happy Christmas, happy Christmas!
Christ is born today.

Lucy (4)

(Lucy was nearly 5 years old when, just before Christmas, her mother heard her describing a picture of the Nativity to her doll. 'I'll sing you a song about that,' she said, and her mother reached quickly for pen and paper.)

A Peculiar Christmas

Snow? Absolutely not.
In fact, the weather's quite hot.
At night you can watch this new
Star without catching the 'flu.

Presents? Well, only three.
But then there happen to be
Only three guests. No bells,
No robins, no fir-trees, no smells

– I mean of roast turkey and such:
There are whiffs in the air (a bit much!)
Of beer from the near public house,
And of dirty old shepherds, and cows.

The family party's rather
Small – baby, mother and father –
Uncles, aunts, cousins dispersed.
Well, this Christmas IS only the first.

Roy Fuller

Birth of a Baby

January 16th, 1991,
Was all set to be an ordinary day,
But the ringing of the phone at seven thirty
Changed that.
For nine months
My step mum had carried a load,
Nine months of feeling
Like a beached whale.
That Wednesday,
Bethany Clare was born.
It was my dad on the phone,
Telling the good news,
"Mother and baby both fit and well."
That night I went to visit.
She was so small,
So delicate,
So harmless.
I held her;
She is beautiful,
My half sister.

Gemma Chilvers (13)

The New Baby

You really are lucky,
it is such a treat,
your new baby brother,
here for you to meet.

Sorry, but don't touch,
you'll poke out his eye.
Oh look now, your faces
have made baby cry.

Don't make a noise now,
baby's asleep.
Turn off the TV,
come and have a peep.

Look at his little face,
no, he's not dead.
Don't tap his rattle,
QUIET! I said.

You've woken the baby.
Oh really, do try.
Why must you do things
that make baby cry?

Don't play trains dear,
put the spaceship away.
Yes, I am certain
that baby *will* stay.

Robin Mellor

Snowman

You must stay here
Till the snow melts away
Into the road.

When the snow comes
I will go into the garden
And make a snowman.
And I will make a snow hand
And hold it.
And I will make snow feet
And he can walk about in the garden.
And when the snow melts,
He will blow away in the wind.

Ben Howison (2 years, 4 months)

(Ben Howison's father – 'This was produced quite spontaneously, and came out all at once with scarcely a pause. I wrote it down immediately and have made no alterations at all.')

Making a Snowman

It must be
the hundredth time
I've made a
snowman –
patted him down
and given
him
a face.

This year,
he's wearing
my old scarf
and bonnet.
He stands and stares,
still
in the same old
place.

His pebble eyes
look
into whitened
distance.
And so do I.
Neither of us
can know
what hour
the sun will choose
to melt and make us
a little less
a little less
    than snow . . .

Jean Kenward

The Pantomime

I remember the zip just
Wouldn't do up quickly enough,
As I pulled on my hand-me-down
Anorak. We were going to see
The Debenham Players!

I stumbled along
The darkened aisle, feeling like
The 'It' in Blind Man's Buff.
We waited, staring at
The silhouetted castle.
Then the curtain rose
And there she was!
Her stagnant-green hair
Protruded from the large black hat,
Planted firmly on her ugly head.
A large boil erupted
From her wrinkled nose.
And tongues of fire seemed to leap
From her finger-tips
As the spotlight flickered
On her witch's claws.
Her scream revealed
A scrap-heap of teeth.
Her piercing eyes had even the boldest
Of the audience silent.

As we filed out of the doors,
I peered around a screen.
There stood an actor;
He was robed in black
And wore a cheap green wig;
Orange plastic nails were sellotaped

To his fingers and he wore
Too much powder on his nose.

'That's funny,' I remember thinking,
'He wasn't in the show.'

Tim Connors (15)

Kids' Show Time-To-Go Poem

We hope that you think our theatre
was better than robbers and cops,
we hope you take something away with you and
we hope it's not one of our props.

John Hegley

Eid

The moon is rising
Ramadan's ended
Eid is here – Hooray!

Mums are cooking
Men are praying
Girls henna their hands – hooray!

Families are gathering
With presents and money
Mum brings us all food – hooray!

Asma Tabassum (12)

Ramadan is the ninth month of the Muslim year, when people fast through the hours of daylight until mahgreb, or dusk. The first sight of the new moon marks the end of the fast and the beginning of the holiday of Eid (sometimes spelt Idh) al-Fitr. Then presents are exchanged, gifts given to charity, and everyone wears new or special clothes to join in the feasting and celebrating.

Idh al-Fitr

In the ninth month of Ramadan, one moon to another,
From sunrise to sunset the true Muslim brother,
For love of his God with a faith everlasting
Is steadfast in prayer and is strict in his fasting.

But come the new moon, Ramadan is then over.
It's Idh al-Fitr and each child is in clover.
The boys all so handsome in thobes of white cotton.
The long hours of school for a while are forgotten.

The girls are so pretty in new party dresses
With bright satin ribbons adorning dark tresses.
The mail-box is bursting with 'Happy Idh' greetings
And daytime is taken with visits and meetings.

The sun sinks to Westward, the Red Sea gets redder
As, dressed like a child-bride, the streets of old Jeddah
Are in festival mood, coloured lights brightly burning
Over beach carousel and the ferris wheel turning.

There's presents for everyone, treats and surprises.
There's gold for the ladies and sweetmeats and spices.
Yet one day it's over. Each heart's a shade sadder.
But wait! – Only two months and it's then Idh al-Adha.

Philip Gross

Rage

The things they said
Gave birth
To a great
Fiery sun that rose in my throat.
My brain
Burnt with angry words.
I ground my nails
Deep into my palm
As if to find and slit
A vein belonging to them.
I stared, amazed – their calm words
Hit me like bullets – and
In my throat the sun burnt, fiercely.
My heart seemed to batter
Itself against my ribs.
War! it yelled. . . .
And then I remembered
Who was saying these words;
And my only answer
Was a tear slipping silently
Down my cheek.

Zoe Cumberland (14)

Family

Cold fear mingles with hot anger
I speak words I never
thought I'd hear
From my own lips
To my own family

Later
Cold anger mingles with hot fear
And shame
But overriding all
Righteous indignation
Which will keep
The row submerged
Under the surface of our lives
Until someone
Sails too far into the shallows
again.

Carol Paten

Pancakes

Mummy made pancakes on Tuesday
She tossed them in the air
One fell on the floor
Two fell on the chair
One fell on the cooker
One fell on the grate
But lucky me I got three
Because they fell on my plate.

Glenn O'Neill (8)

Pancake Day

Mix a pancake,
Stir a pancake,
Pop it in the pan;
Fry the pancake,
Toss the pancake –
Catch it if you can.

Christina Rossetti

Pancake Day, also known as Shrove Tuesday, is the day before the beginning of Lent, when Christians used not to eat any meat or rich foods for six weeks. To get rid of all the eggs and fat in the house, before the fast began, they cooked them up into a feast of pancakes.

Thoughts from a Dentist's Waiting Room

Please let there be a powercut.
Just a tiny little one.
Just before he gets the drill near my mouth.

One down, two to go

Or maybe he'll be struck down,
By a hitherto undiscovered and as yet incurable
palsy
which only lasts for the ten minutes I'm with him,
and then vanishes forever?

Two down, one to go

Maybe he got the notes mixed up.
'Ridiculous,' he'll say, 'You don't need fillings at all!'
'They're old Mrs Crabtree's notes!' (even though
she has dentures).

NEXT PLEASE!

Why is the dentist the only one who is ever smiling?

Amanda Evans (14)

At the Dentist

A kindly smile from reception;
Hear my own voice; 'Nice day today.'
'Take a seat, won't keep you waiting.'

> Please God, can't you call him away?
> Or arrange a small brief power-cut?
> 'Apologies; We're running late,
> Shall I revise your appointment?'
> 'Yes please, another (far off) date.'

Pick up a Punch, very ancient;
Pretend that I'm being amused;
Reach for a thick Home and Country
And find myself pinned and confused
By the gaze of a small serious child
Her hand in her mother's clutched tight,
The mother sitting silent beside her.
(Unaware of those knuckles clenched white?)
The little girl gravely surveys me
Her brown eyes absorbent and clear.
Does she know? This big grown-up man
Feels the same sharp stabs of fear?

Bob Sparrow

Holi, the Coming of Spring

The most colourful festival
Of the Hindus,
And the coming of Spring.

People of all ages
Flick coloured powders at each other.
We duck and hide, sing and dance.

Our mothers fast until the evening,
And pray for their children's
Safety for ever.

In the evening the hungry mothers,
And all the rest of us,
Feed on mouthwatering food.

Rakhi Unadkat (10)

Holi is a happy Spring festival when Hindus honour the Lord Krishna. Krishna was a mischievous god who loved tricks and games. When Hindus celebrate him they imitate his playfulness by chasing, and flicking coloured waters and powders at each other.

Garaba

Dressed in bright saris
Elaborated with gold and
Silver thread or
Dashed with sequins
We dance,
A shimmering ring.

The footweary
And the old
And, of course, the men
Whose feet have never
Heard the beat,
Stand chatting,
Drinking squash while
Dreaming of fresh mango
And lime.

A school hall
In a land of
Perpetual winter
Can never be India
But the song
Is of Krishna, god
Of our dance
And our hearts.

Carol Paten

Garaba is a dance performed at Holi and also at Daśahara, after the monsoon rains.

Birthdays

At nine months
My life was confused,
Amid screams and blood
I was born.

Although with little understanding,
I enjoyed my birthday
At three
On piles of card and paper
I slept smiling.

When I was seven
My party was a thrill
Of oranges and sherbet,
Musical statues and
A cake full of candles.

By ten, birthdays had become serious.
Ordered swimming trips replaced
Riotous, unregulated tumbles.
My own satisfaction lost through
Concern for others' pleasure.

And now that day passes
Quietly, semi-forgotten.
At fifteen I plough through homework
Deserted by my party friends
And the candles
Too numerous
Are extinguished.

Adam Stanley (15)

Birthdays

My friend has a birthday;
And what can I say
To young Betty Blake
With her wonderful cake
And seven pink candles there –
One candle for every year?
'How many candles shall I see
On yours?' asked Betty Blake of me.
'Sixty!' I cried, excited by it –
Steady, old heart! Lie quiet!

W.H. Davies

My Bird Peter

My bird was yellow,
And my brother killed it.
It is in our back garden,
And it was gorgeous.

And I want it,
Because I liked it,
Because it was my bird.
It could stand on the tele.
It was funny.
It did do funny things.

Then it did love my mummy.

When it died it was only five.
Our David did not like it,
Because his tail kept going in his nose.
So he got this knife and he stabbed it.

I battered him.
I kicked him in the leg.
Me and my mum went to the pet shop,
And we will get another one next week.

Sarah Taylor (6)

The Dead Bird

'Is it quite dead?'
They asked, gravely,
Tenderly holding the dusty feathered body
In dirty, gentle hands.

'Will it come alive again?'
Asked the younger,
Caressing the neat grey-green feathers,
Unfolding the tiny claws.

'No. We must bury it,'
Said the elder,
And scooped a grave in the dry earth,
Neat, and bird-small.

'I must be sure,'
Thought the younger,
Quietly uncovering the small corpse again;
But it was quite dead.

Sylvia Hodgkinson

Mother's Day Musings

Blast Mother's day!
The costly card,
The refrigerated rose
And worst of all
The breakfast in bed
soggy sausage
burnt bacon
And scrunchy puffs,
all un-scrunchy
Blast Mother's day!

Michelle Bennett (11)

In the United Kingdom, Mothering Sunday is the middle Sunday in Lent. It used to be a special holiday, when children who lived away from home as apprentices, or 'in service', were allowed to go back to see their parents for the day. Often they took little gifts of flowers, violets or primroses, to give to their mothers.

In the United States of America, Mother's Day is a newly invented festival, celebrated on the second Sunday of May. But the idea behind it is the same. Children give their mothers presents and cards, and perhaps a special treat like breakfast in bed, to thank them for their care on every other day of the year.

Mothering Sunday

In the times before Bank Holidays
Farmer's boys and servant girls
Left the farm or big house early,
Going home for the day
On Mothering Sunday
Though home was miles away,
With flowers for their mother's present
Gathered as they went.

It's different these days:
All you have to do is stop
At the flower shop
With the pocket money you've saved
And the daffodils there
Came by train or even by plane;
But the present still means the same
For the language of flowers doesn't change.

Stanley Cook

Playground Fight

It was me and him,
I charged,
he ducked,
I ran into a brick wall,
I bounced back,
and hit him on the head,
he fell to the floor,
I squashed him,
I took him home,
and put him through the letter box,
because he was flat.
The next day he came back,
flat as a pancake,
he wobbled,
he became himself again,
he charged,
I stuck out my fist,
he ran into it . . .
the Head Master came,
we got detention.

Raymond Trott (10)

Playground Fight

How did your coat get so dirty?
How come the hood is unstitched?
You must have been through a hedge backwards
Or sat in a ditch?
Why is Nasim's mother glaring?
You haven't been having a fight?
Don't tell me it starts in the playground
As soon as your mum's out of sight?
Why is Tom's mother pointing?
I can tell there is something not right.
You told me you *hadn't* been fighting . . .
. . . But, son, a 'scrap' *is* a fight!

Celia Warren

April Fool's Day

April Fool's Day's round once more
The same old jokes cracked yet again,
'Oh look, an elephant there outside!
Fooled you! Fooled you!'

For a change this year, it was at school.
Assembly as usual, then something strange.
Our teacher had an official letter.
'Dear Sir or Madam,' it read,

'We regret to inform you, your school
Will have to put in three extra hours
Each week, either after school, or
On a Saturday morning.'

'HELP!' we all thought,
'I can't do Saturdays, or Sundays either.'
'And I can't do Tuesdays or Thursdays
After school.' 'Nor me.' 'Nor me.'

We went through all our options,
Discussing every one.
Then suddenly our teachers shouted,
'April Fools, the lot of you!'

Amy Kieran (13)

The 1st April is April Fool's Day, sometimes called All Fools' Day. People play tricks and try to make fools of each other. But at 12 o'clock, mid-day, the fooling has to stop, otherwise the trickster is considered the fool.

Good News

The Board of Education has just set up new rules
That in the future they'll shut all the schools
On every April Fool's.

APRIL FOOL!
(Keep cool.)

William Cole

Lost

Huge tall shapes
Loom around,
I can't see the sky,
Only the ground.
A forest of legs
Pinning me in,
Bumping my head,
Kicking my shin.

Nobody sees me
Down here on the floor,
I can't see my mother,
I can't see the door.
I'll just have to stand here
Till Mummy gets back,
Shoes all around me
Go clickety-clack.

I see something familiar
Walking straight by.
My mother's blue trainers!
So I call out, 'Hi!
Mummy, it's me,
Down here on the floor!'
They carry on walking
Straight to the door.

I stand up and yell
At the top of my lungs.
There's a ladder before me
And through the rungs
I can see my Mum running
Faster than light.
I hurl myself at her
With all of my might.

I'm SAFE!

Erica Heatly (12)

64

Small Incident in Library

The little girl is lost among the books.
Two years old maybe, in bobble cap,
White lacy tights, red coat. She stands and looks.
'Can't see you, Mummy.' Mummy, next row up,
Intent on reading answers absently:
'I'm here, love.' Child calls out again: 'Can't see.'

A large man, his intentions of the best,
Stoops: 'Where's Mummy, then?' Child backs away.
Now the tall shelves threaten like a forest.
She toddles fast between them, starts to cry,
Takes the next aisle down and as her mother
Rounds one end disappears behind the other.

I catch the woman's tired-eyed prettiness.
We smile, shake heads. The child comes back in sight,
Hurtles to her laughing, hugs her knees:
'Found you!', in such ringing pure delight
It fills the room, there's no one left who's reading.
The mother looks down, blinking. 'Great soft thing.'

David Sutton

The Real Bully

Why does he REALLY do it?
  I REALLY don't know.
Personally I hate him.
  I REALLY do.
He's REALLY bad to people.
  I REALLY think so.
He REALLY pushes people around,
  That's what I don't like
I just wish he could be –
  Well I'm not being nasty
but I would REALLY enjoy it,
  If I saw him bashed around.
  I REALLY would
  By someone HUGE
  REALLY, REALLY H-U-G-E.

Paul Robinson (12)

Bullies

With the eye in the back of his head
he sees them coming –

eight-year-old breakers,
baby-hard, baby-soft.

Their space-machine, so elegant
could swallow him,

drown him once and for all
in a dish of air.

No use trying to rewrite the law:
they are the masters –

skills bred in the bone.
He freezes –

they expect it,
though a voice inside him squeaks

I . . . Words cut his tongue,
weigh in his mind like a bruise.

Katherine Gallagher

Our Visit to the Zoo

(by 3A4, who 'borrowed' the first verse and invented the others)

We went to the Zoo
We saw a gnu
An elk and a whelk
And a wild kangaroo.

We saw a giraffe
Whose neck made us laugh,
And a whale flip his tail
Whilst taking a bath.

We saw a seal
Who was eating his meal,
Of a fish from a dish,
With a joyful squeal.

We saw a white rabbit
That had a bad habit,
His nose twitched and snitched,
As a boy tried to grab it.

We saw a bear
Covered in fur,
And a skunk that stunk
But didn't care.

We saw a snake
That was hardly awake
And a lion eat meat
They'd forgotten to bake.

We saw a cockatoo
Creating a to-do,
We saw an ape eat a grape
And a big banana too.

We saw a zoo keeper
Attacked by a cheetah,
And a mouse in its house
Keeping warm by a heater.

At the end of the day
We wanted to stay
But 'Sir' didn't care
And he drove us away.

Group Work (13)

A Visit to the Zoo

Now then children, form a queue
Let me count you going through
27, 29; Daphne darling, stay in line
30, 31 & 2; Sandra, where's your other shoe?
Leave your knickers Pam my pet
Take them *off* then if they're wet!
Hands up those who need the loo
Off you go then. Follow Prue.
Wendy! Mandy! NOT IN THERE!!
That's the GENTS you dozy pair.
Donna dear, you can't stroke that
That's no ordinary cat.
Blow your nose Ann, don't just sniff.
Sue your hat is on skew-whiff.
No, the parrot doesn't swear
You provoke him if you dare.
Hilary! For heaven's sake
Who pushed Cathy in the lake?
O-oh Yvonne, my tiny friend
Elephants eat at the *other* end.
Come along now. Time for lunch
Settle down you noisy bunch.
Dilys, don't you want to eat?
Child! You're whiter than a sheet!
What's that darling, Abigail's
Got her head stuck in the rails!
Fetch the keeper someone. Quick!
(Rotten kids, they make me sick)
Keeper, *don't* just stand and grin
Open a cage and put me in!

J.J. Webster

Father's Day

Father's Day is when
You should be kind to
Your Dad
And get him a card or a present
Or if you are VERY kind
You could get him
Both.
Father's Day is the one
Day of the year when
You should respect
Your Dad.

Josiah Paten (9)

Father's Day is a new invention. It is celebrated in the middle of June, and is a chance to say thank you to our fathers just as, on Mother's Day, we say thank you to our mothers.

70

My Father's Day Card

'Commercialism, that's all it is,
The world's gone mad,' I'd say,
Until at last *I* got a card –
The sun came out that day!

Timothy Sherwood

Supermarket Speeding

Yeah, quick, grab a trolley!
I'll beat ya to the checkout –
Beep brrrm beep brrrm brrrrm beep
speeding round the corner
through the toy department
dodge the old lady
clear the baby
There's my brother but
he can't catch me oh yeah oh yeah –
there are the cheeses up on the straight
stacking on the corner
no time to brake oh no oh no
There's an old man standing
he's bending down
so I hit him in the head oh yeah oh yeah
he's dead
Down the chocolate
up the frozen food
There is my mum
now I'm a sad dude oh yeah oh yeah
she gives me half an inch,
and I'm speeding away
through the stationery
through the books
another minute later I hit the sonic boom oh yeah
    oh yeah
I'm going too fast and I'm trying to stop
next thing ya know
I'm burning up, oh yeah, oh yeah.

Damian Elvin (11)

Supermarket Shopping

It is good to have help with the shopping.
My son was quite keen to assist.
So he left off his practising cricket
And offered to carry my list.

The first thing we saw was the fruit;
He would choose me an orange, he said.
Next thing I knew he was overarm-bowling,
Narrowly missing my head.

He did not let go of the orange
Until it was safe in the trolley,
By then he was at the sweet counter
And trying to bat with a lolly.

He seemed to be scoring some runs
But I saw from the look on the face
Of the man who was stocking the counters
That this really was not the right place.

He succeeded in stumping an egg-box.
He said it was 'Out for a duck!'
Not even one egg was broken,
But I still reckon that was just luck.

He told me the Delicatessen
Was the boundary where he would score six,
Then he swiped an invisible ball in the air
With the last of the crusty french sticks.

I was glad when we got to the check-out
And he seemed to have done with his bat.
If only I'd not dropped that bottle of squash
He would never have shouted, 'Howzat!'

Celia Warren

73

The Camouflage Hat

One Monday morning,
At primary school,
We were off to the museum.
'Has everyone got a packed lunch?'
The teacher said,
In her flowered dress
And brown sandals.
'Line up in twos.'
There was a huddle in the corner
Arguing about who was going with who.
A sudden silence filled the room;
The headmaster came in,
A camouflage hat on his head.
A small boy had an urge to laugh.
We joined in.
A shout, a roar, an explosion of anger
Stormed out of the headmaster.
'How dare you!'
There was quiet again.
'Sorry, sir, sorry.'

Donna Keeble (12)

Recipe for a Class Outing

Ingredients:
30 children, washed and scrubbed
29 packed lunches (no bottles)
3 teachers
an equal quantity of mums
1 nosebleed
2 fights
a hot day
3 lost purses
1 slightly torn dress
plenty of sweets
5 or 6 songs (optional)

Method:
Place children and adults in a bus and heat slowly.
Season well with sweets, reserving a few for later.
Heat to boiling point. Add fights and nosebleed.
Leave to simmer for 2 hours.
Remove children and packed lunches and leave to cool.
Stir in torn dress and lost purses.
Return to heat, add songs to taste.
Mix thoroughly. If the children go soggy and start to
    stick together, remove from the bus and drain.
At the end of the cooking time divide into individual
    portions (makes about 36).
Serve with relief, garnished liberally with dirt.

Sue Cowling

Car Crash

A screech of brakes,
A crunch of cars
And silence broke out.
I rolled forwards.
Helpless and alone,
Cut and weak,
I lay in darkness.

A deafening siren
Pierced my ears.

Later, lying in white,
I was a stranger
In a strange
But safe world.

Kate Kydd (11)

Tulips for Ness

Don't embarrass me by crying
You said, as we walked
Arm in arm
Down the disinfected corridor.
I wept outside
In the bleary light.
Next day your face lay fragile
On the white pillow,
Your arm stitched and plastered,
Immobile at your side,
Your tears frail as buds
On the stem of your pain,
As I touched you,
Murmured your name.

Theresa Heine

Sports Day

Oh no! My race next.
We're all in a line.
I'm about to be sick.
Now the count down,
O-o-o-n-n your marks,
G-e-e-t-t- set,
Go!

And we're off.

First of all my friend is in the lead,
Then I'm catching up on her,
We're getting equal,
Now I've got the edge,
I'm away on my own,
Down on the finish,
Two more steps to go,
I look around,
I'm way ahead,
The last step.

A-a-n-d-d I've finished.

Phew! What a race, what a lead.
It must have been a record.
Wow! it IS a record!
All I can hear in the background
Is the loud speaker
Shouting the news. What a win!

Grace Mason (14)

Sports Day!

Now you mustn't worry,
it won't be like last year.
This time I'm prepared,
even got all the gear.

I know last sports day
there was a bit of an alarm.
But I couldn't help falling
and breaking my arm!

Now you must understand,
the family pride is at stake.
But this time – no slip-up,
trip up or silly mistake.

Yes I've done all the sweating,
I've done all the training.
My tracksuit is bulging,
my muscles are straining.

Everything's been streamlined,
I've EVEN lost weight.
Just stand back and watch me
takeoff – accelerate.

So off to the finish
and watch out for first place,
it's time for me to take part
in the school fathers' race.

Ian Souter

First Day of the Holidays

It's early.

    My body is heavy and relaxed.
      My tousled head, warm in the hollow of the pillow.
      My eyes feel delightfully fresh and cool.

It's excitement.

    A bubbling underground spring,
      longing to burst free,
        to express effervescently the undiscovered.

It's ecstasy.

      Like the birth of a sneeze.
        The sparkling crest of a yawn.
        The calm after spasms
          of perpetual hiccups.

I stretch.
    And throw wide my sunfilled curtains
          of happiness.

Nikki Field (13)

Summer Holidays – For Parent

The first day of Summer –
Tired mother-and-dadness,
Of teeth-gritted weeping,
Of six weeks of terror,
Of six weeks of horror,
Of six weeks of sorrow,
No hope for tomorrow –

Until (must remember)
A bright new September!

John Kitching

Badger Watching with Gran

Black all over
Two white stripes on his forehead
Triangly shaped head
Oval shaped body
Sharp claws
Furry
White at the tip of his tail
It's a badger!

Sam Henry (7)

Badger Watching with Sam

The question was quiet. 'Would you like
to watch badgers?' The sight
of your eyes, opening wider and rounder,
supplied a clear answer.

'And could you keep still, motionless, silent,
awake in the dark, and count to a thousand?'
You wondered, and tried it, nodding your head
until you decided.

As we walked through the field, with dew on our
     trousers,
the red sky grew gradually dark.
When we heard the owls hoot
you held my hand hard.

Under the oaks the darkness was nearer.
We crept between trees and heard each twig snap.
Settled beneath them we noticed new spaces
where angular branches fingered the stars.

We sat close together, cosy in blankets,
to stare into tunnels badgers had dug.
Your jacket made squeaks in time to your heartbeat.
I swivelled my eyes without moving my head.

It did not take long. I knew you were counting.
The shape of a hole changed; a pale edge appeared.
I twitched and you stiffened; we both stopped
     breathing –
a badger, two badgers were suddenly there.

They ran by your feet, so close they could touch you,
black and white cushions, unrolling themselves
from under the ground, sniffing for night food
upwind of our smell.

When gaps between trees disappeared into darkness
what made the rustling was harder to tell.
While the badgers were busy all night with their
     business
we went home to bed, and slept, with their smell.

                                        Jane Whittle

The Weather Forecast

'It may rain tomorrow,'
The man on the radio said.
'It may rain tomorrow
While you're in bed.'

We're off to the seaside tomorrow,
At least that's what Dad said.
But if it rains tomorrow
We'll stay at home instead.

I hope that it rains when I'm sleeping
Like the man on the radio said.
I hope that it rains while I'm sleeping
Snug and warm in my bed.

I hope that the sun shines tomorrow,
While we're at the seaside as Dad said.
I hope that the sun shines tomorrow,
So we don't have to stay home
instead.

The morning has come and it's sunny.
It rained while I was in bed.
So we're off to the seaside this day,
So blow what the weather man said.

Charles Talbot (8)

Frolic

The children were shouting together
And racing along the sands,
A glimmer of dancing shadows,
A dovelike flutter of hands.

The stars were shouting in heaven,
The sun was chasing the moon:
The game was the same as the children's,
They danced to the self-same tune.

The whole of the world was merry,
One joy from the vale to the height,
Where the blue woods of twilight encircled
The lovely lawns of the light.

George Russell

Learning

The children ran
Into an empty field,
A yellow kite banging against a knee.
Cries of 'It won't go!' and 'No wind!'
Cut through the air,
As they vainly tried the launch.

'Maybe it needs to be bigger.'
'Or smaller.'
'How about a longer tail?'
'What about some bows?'
'You know what they say: trial and error.'
'Mainly error.'
'Never mind; there's always tomorrow.'

The children ran
Into an empty field,
A yellow kite banging against a knee.
Cries of 'We've done it!' and 'It's there!'
Soared through the air,
And the kite soared even higher.

Victoria Parkins (13)

Shout

Shout child, shout!
Stray from the beaten ways
And laugh out;
Sing and spring
While you can;
Can-can and dance and prance in the sun;
Son, shine and run;
Fly your voice,
Fly your kite,
Fly your life!

Keith Armstrong

Acknowledgements

The editor and publishers would like to thank the following for permission to use copyright material in this collection. Every effort has been made to trace copyright holders and we would be grateful to hear from anyone who has been missed out.

National Exhibition of Children's Art for 'First Day at School' by Melanie Louise Skipper, 'Being Stuck in Goal' by Paul Oliffe, 'My Grandad' by Matthew Lea, 'Rockets' by Jonathan Brown, 'Going To Tea With Grandma' by Alexandra Calvert, 'Christmas Joy' by Helen Robinson, 'Gone' by Ellen Jackson, 'Thoughts From A Dentist's Waiting Room' by Amanda Evans, 'Birthdays' by Adam Stanley, 'My Bird Peter' by Sarah Taylor, 'Mother's Day Musings' by Michelle Bennett, 'The Real Bully' by Paul Robinson, 'Our Visit to the Zoo' (Group Work), 'First Day of the Holidays' by Nikki Field and 'A Day At The Sea' by Charles Talbot.

Ann Bonner for 'First Day' and 'Grandchild', copyright the poet.

Andrew Storer for 'First Lesson', copyright the poet, of Debenham High School.

Heinemann for 'Esmé on her Brother's Bicycle' by Russell Hoban, from *The Pedalling Man* by Russell Hoban, 'Hallowe'en' by Dawn Elizabeth Edwards from *Children As Writers 2*.

David Phipps for 'Lovely Tracey', copyright the poet.

Random House Children's Books for 'Growing Pain' by Vernon Scannell, from *Love Shouts and Whispers* by Vernon Scannell.

Sarah Ainsworth for 'A Swimming Song', copyright the poet.

Philip Booth for 'First Lesson', copyright the poet.

Depal Patel for 'Firework Festival', copyright the poet, of St Cedd's School.

Oxford University Press for 'Divali' by David Harmer, and 'Idh al-Fitr' by Philip Gross, from *Let's Celebrate* ed. John Foster, 'Firework Night' by Eric Simpson, from *Every Man Will Shout* ed. Roger Mansfield and Isobel Armstrong.

Gina Douthwaite for 'One Girl To Nil', from *Our Side of the Playground* ed. Tony Bradman, published by Bodley Head.

John Rice for 'Hallowe'en Games', copyright the poet.

John Kitching for 'Your Grandad Died', 'Summer Holidays – For Parent' and 'Split Family', copyright the poet.

Laura Walker for 'Hanukkah, The Festival of Oil', copyright the poet, from St Cedd's School.

Celia Warren for 'Candles Burning', 'Playground Fight' and 'Supermarket Shopping', copyright the poet.

OUP Melbourne for 'Christmas Pageant' by Margaret Fishback and 'The Dead Bird' by Sylvia Hodgkinson, from *Celery Noise and Quiet Cheese* compiled by Diana Schafer and Cheryl Irving.

Index of authors

Index of titles

Index of first lines